Aa
Bb
Dd
Ee
Ff
Gg
Hh
Ii
Jj
Kk
Ll
Mm
Nn
Oo
Pp
Qq
Rr
Ss
Tt
Uu
Vv
Ww
Xx
Yy
Zz

Zip

Zip is a friendly space alien from planet Zee. He loves to learn. Zip uses his hands to speak to his friends. He can't wait to teach the people of planet Earth all about sign language. Zip is the captain of his spaceship.

Pella

Pella is Zip's best friend. She also comes from planet Zee. Pella is very brave. Although she is a little younger than Zip and Statz, she isn't afraid of anything and is always the first of the three friends to try new things.

Statz

Statz is in charge of computers on the spaceship. He loves gadgets. Statz uses his Zablet to help him and his friends out of sticky situations. He is excited to learn about planet Earth and all the people who live here.

Goober

Goober is an unexpected guest on the friends' adventures. A greedy and naughty space stowaway, Goober has the ability to change his colour and shape so is always jumping out and surprising Zip, Pella and Statz.

Zip's top tips

Zip and friends are here to help you talk in a fun new way - spell with your fingers and talk with your hands. Follow these top tips to get the most from their adventures:

- **Share the book together and enjoy the story**
- **Play with the signs**
- **Use Zip's alphabet to make your own words**
- **Visit Space School, enjoy the activities and have fun**
- **Watch out for Goober...**

SignSpell

Zip at the Seaside

The spaceship has landed on top of a big sand dune. Zip, Pella and Statz are spending a day at the seaside. They open the spaceship door and tumble out onto the soft sand below.

"Sorry for the bumpy landing everyone!" says Zip.

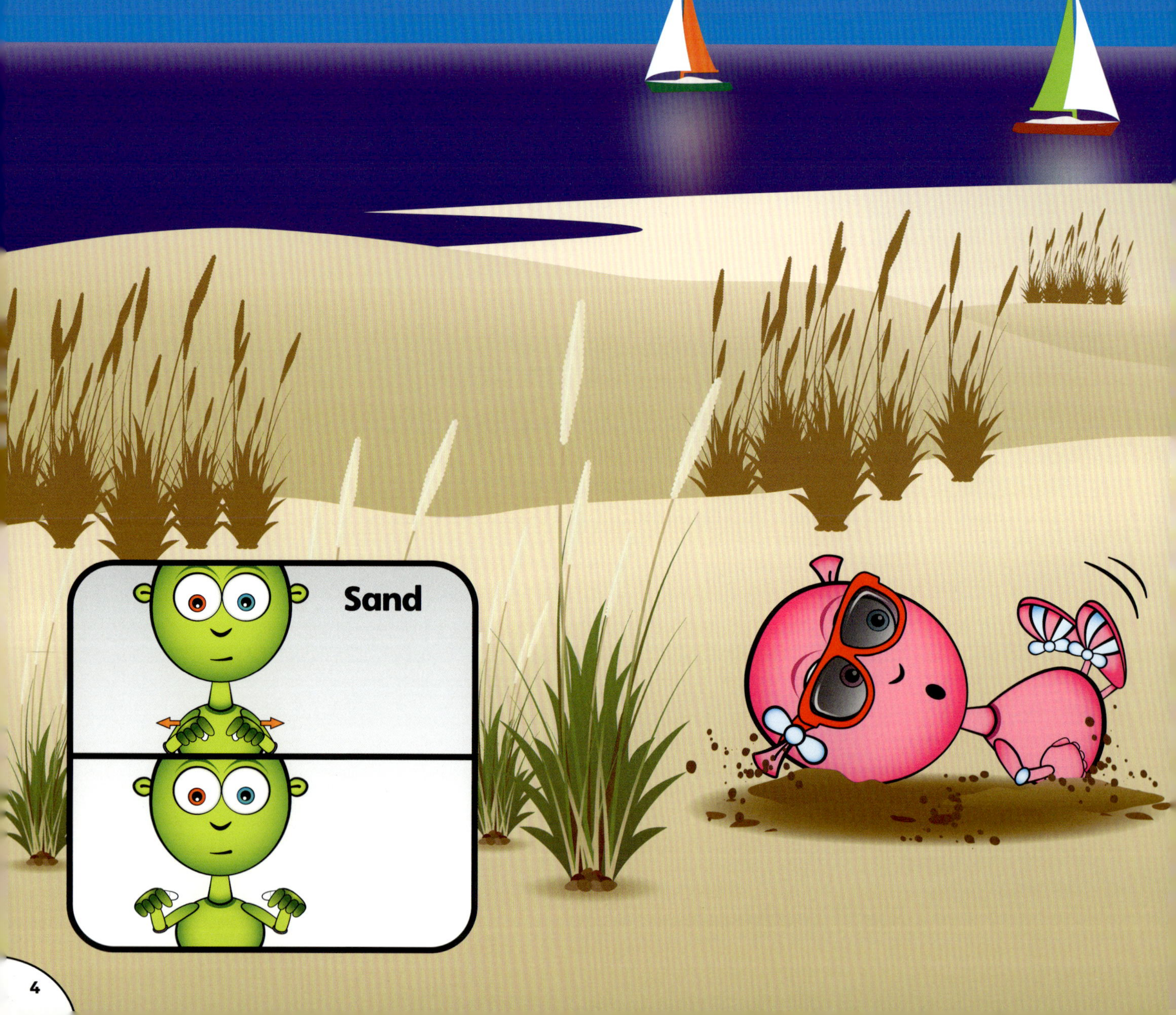

The friends have packed everything they need for a fun day at the beach. Zip has his bucket and spade. Pella has fishing nets and sun cream. Statz loads some beach games onto his Zablet.

"I hope your Zablet is sand-proof Statz!" laughs Pella.

Sun Cream

Statz can't wait to go swimming.

"Last one in the sea is a spikeygog," says Statz.

Zip, Pella and Statz all run down the beach as fast as they can and jump straight in the sea.

Sea

The friends play in the waves, but the sea is cold and soon Zip and Pella have turned blue. “Brrr! The sea on planet Earth is freezing!” says Zip.

Pella’s teeth are chattering. “We...look...just...like...Statz,” she says.

The sun is shining brightly.

Back on the beach Zip, Pella and Statz sunbathe, and soon warm up again.

Zip wants to explore. “There are some rock pools over there,” he says. “Let’s explore.”

The friends grab their fishing nets.

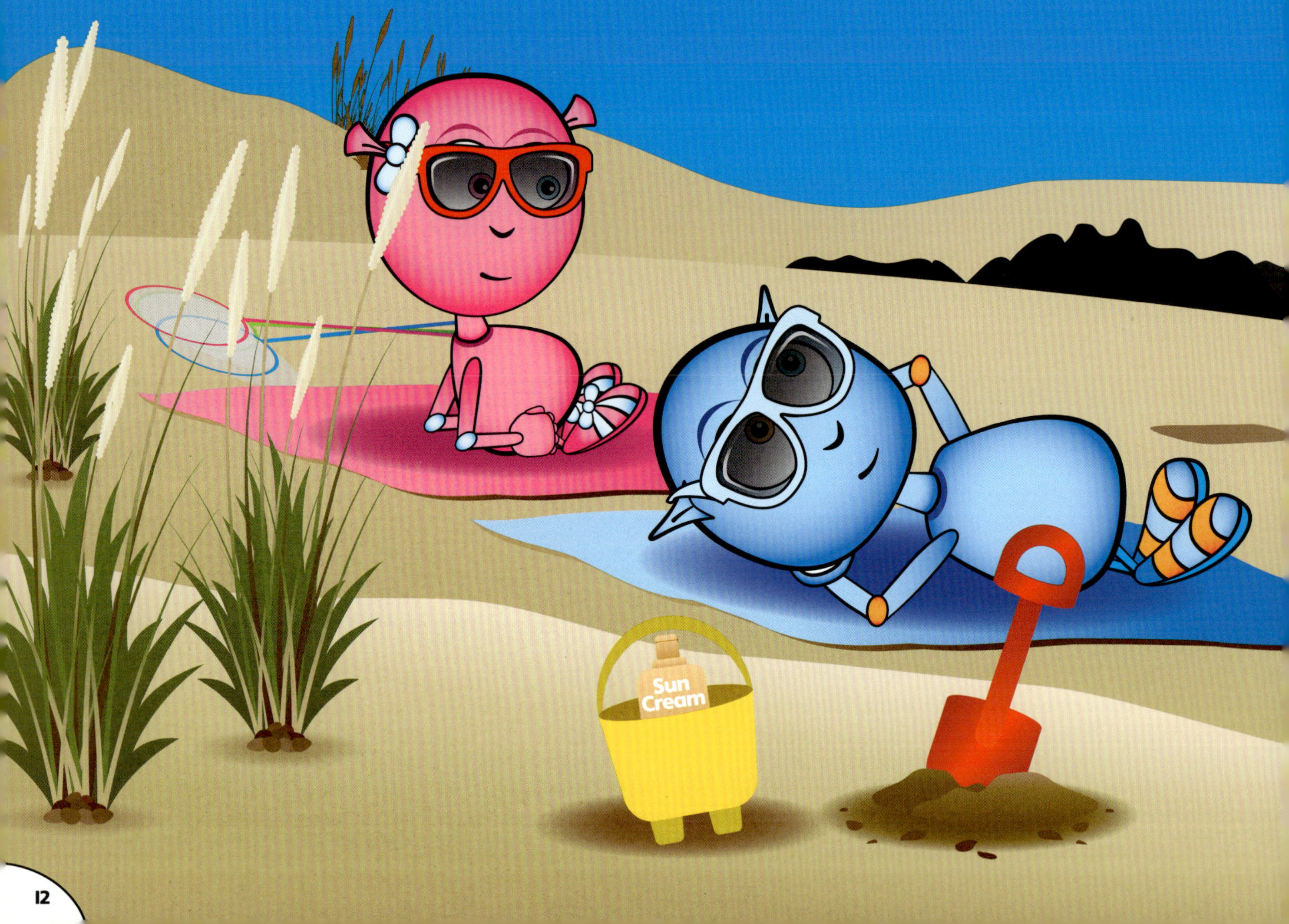

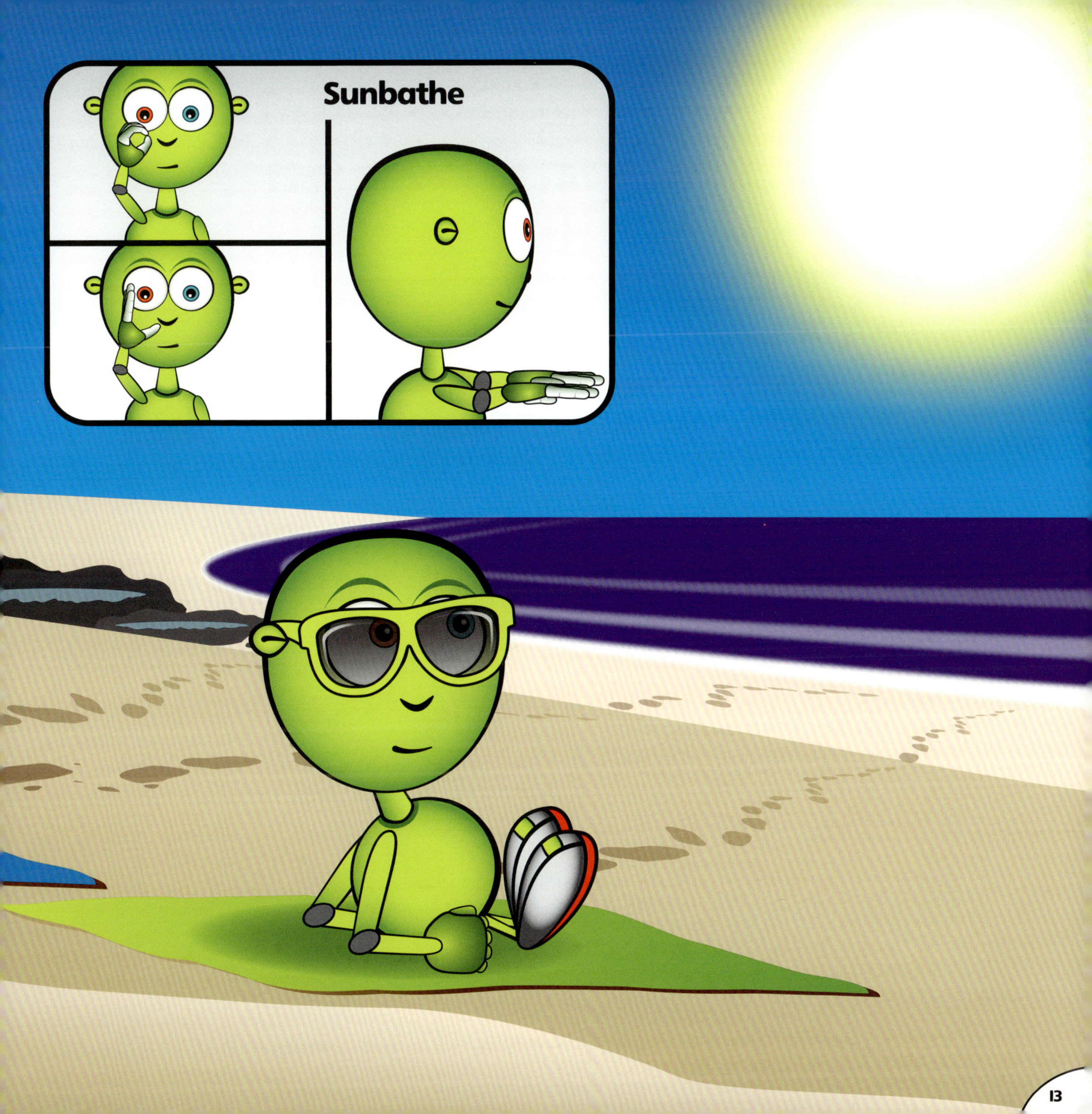
Sunbathe

Zip, Pella and Statz step carefully around the slippery rock pools. In the shallow water they see fish, crabs and starfish. They dip their nets in the water and fish around.

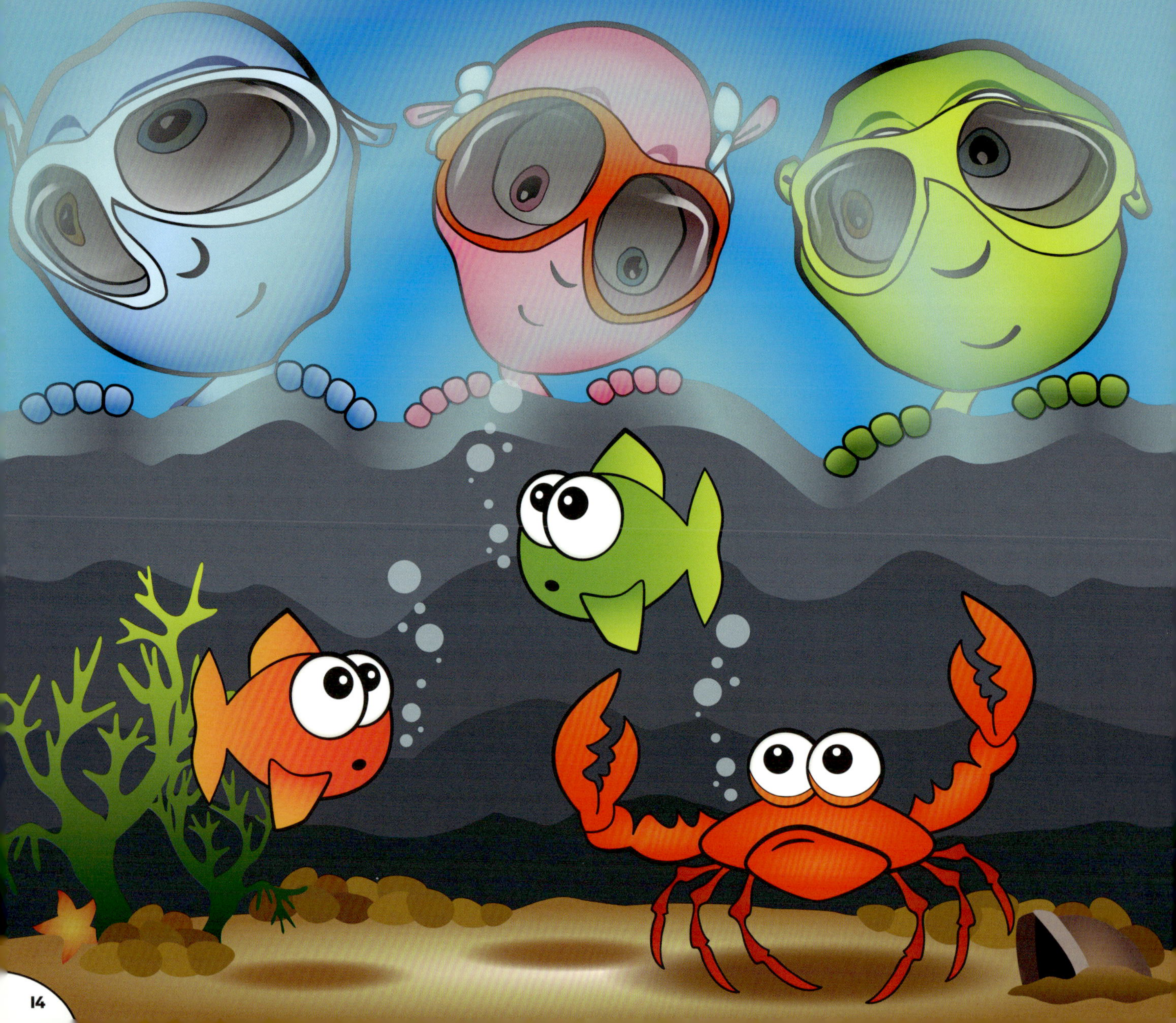

"I've caught something," says Pella. A green fish flips and wriggles in her net.
Statz has caught a crab with big snappy claws.

Zip is not happy. He has caught nothing but an old brown boot.

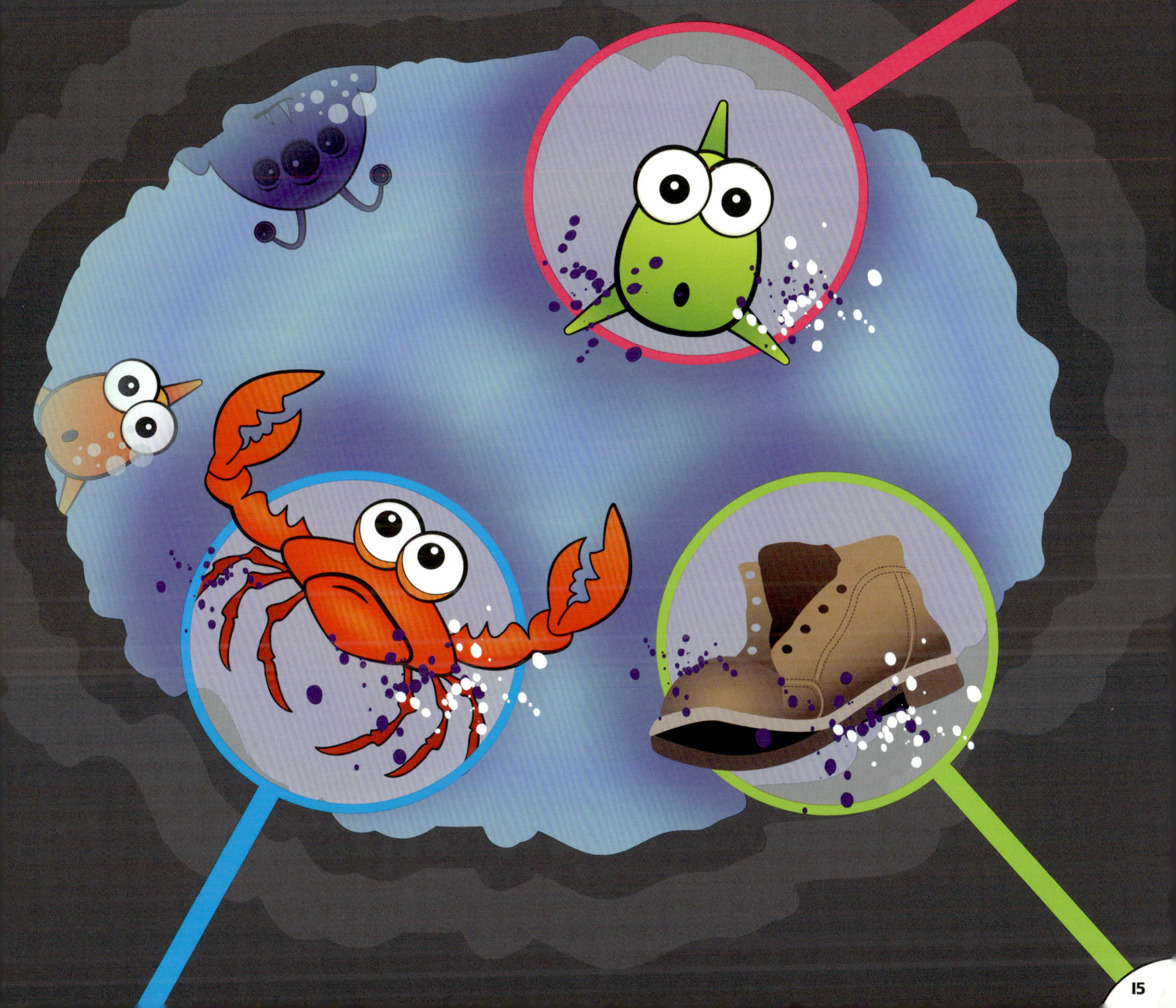

Space School

Take a look at the pictures below; you may have seen them in the story.
See if you can spell each one using Zip's alphabet?

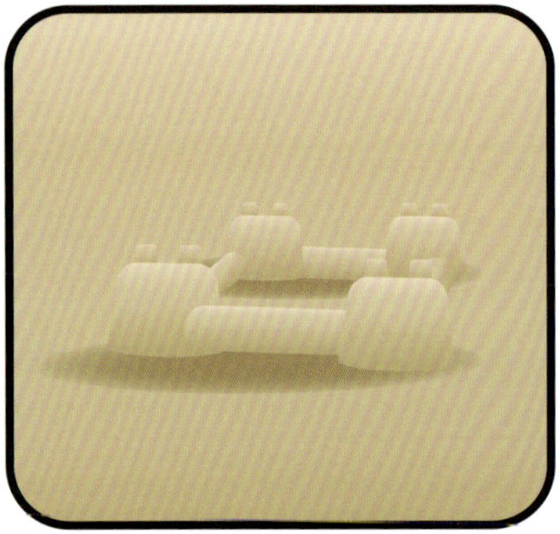

Pella and Statz carefully let the fish and the crab swim back into the rock pool. "I bet that boot belonged to a pirate," says Pella.

"Yes," says Statz, "he only needed one boot because all pirates have one wooden leg."

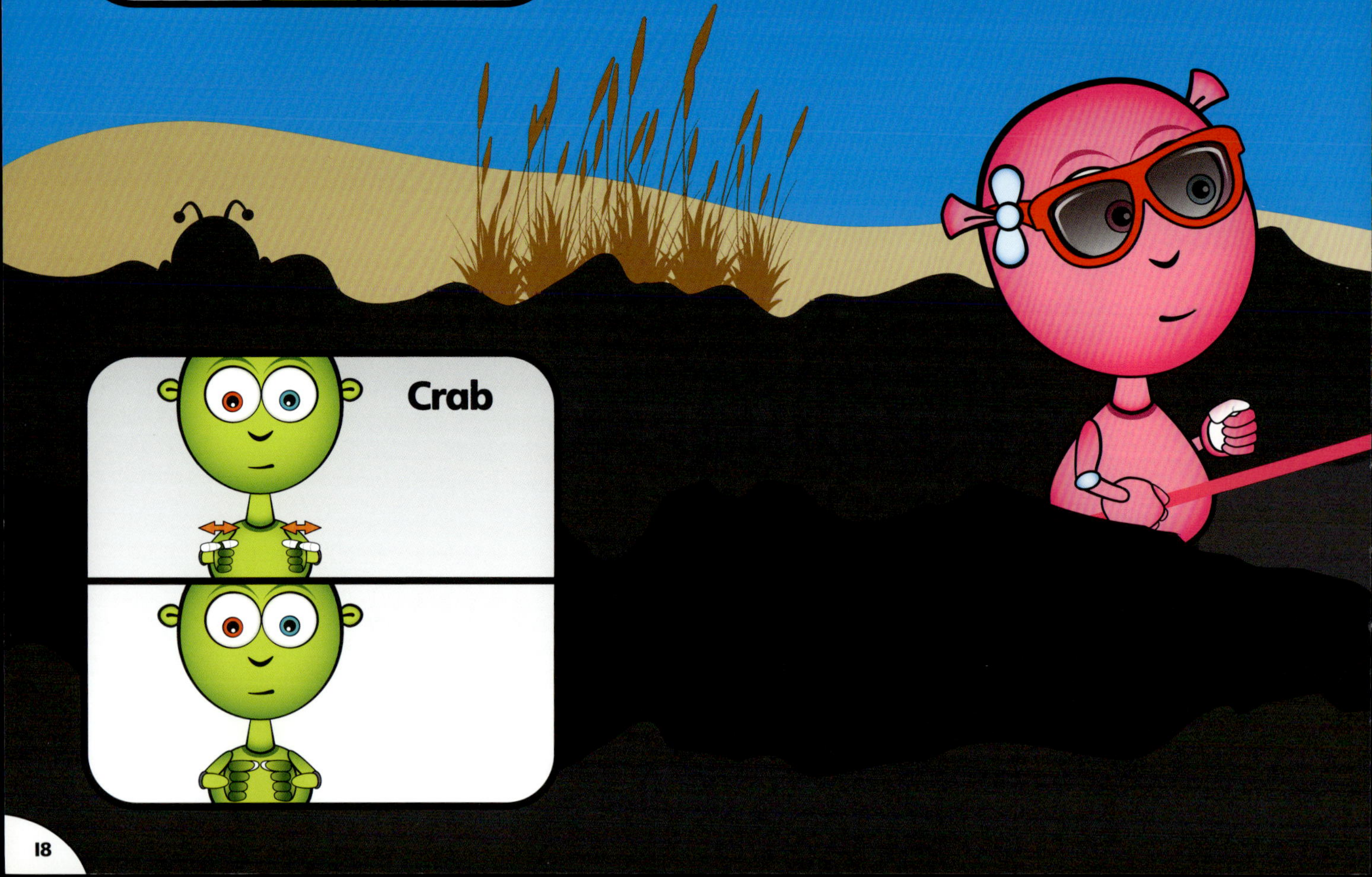

Zip is excited by the thought that pirates once roamed on this beach. “Come on,” he says to his friends, “let’s hunt for buried treasure!”

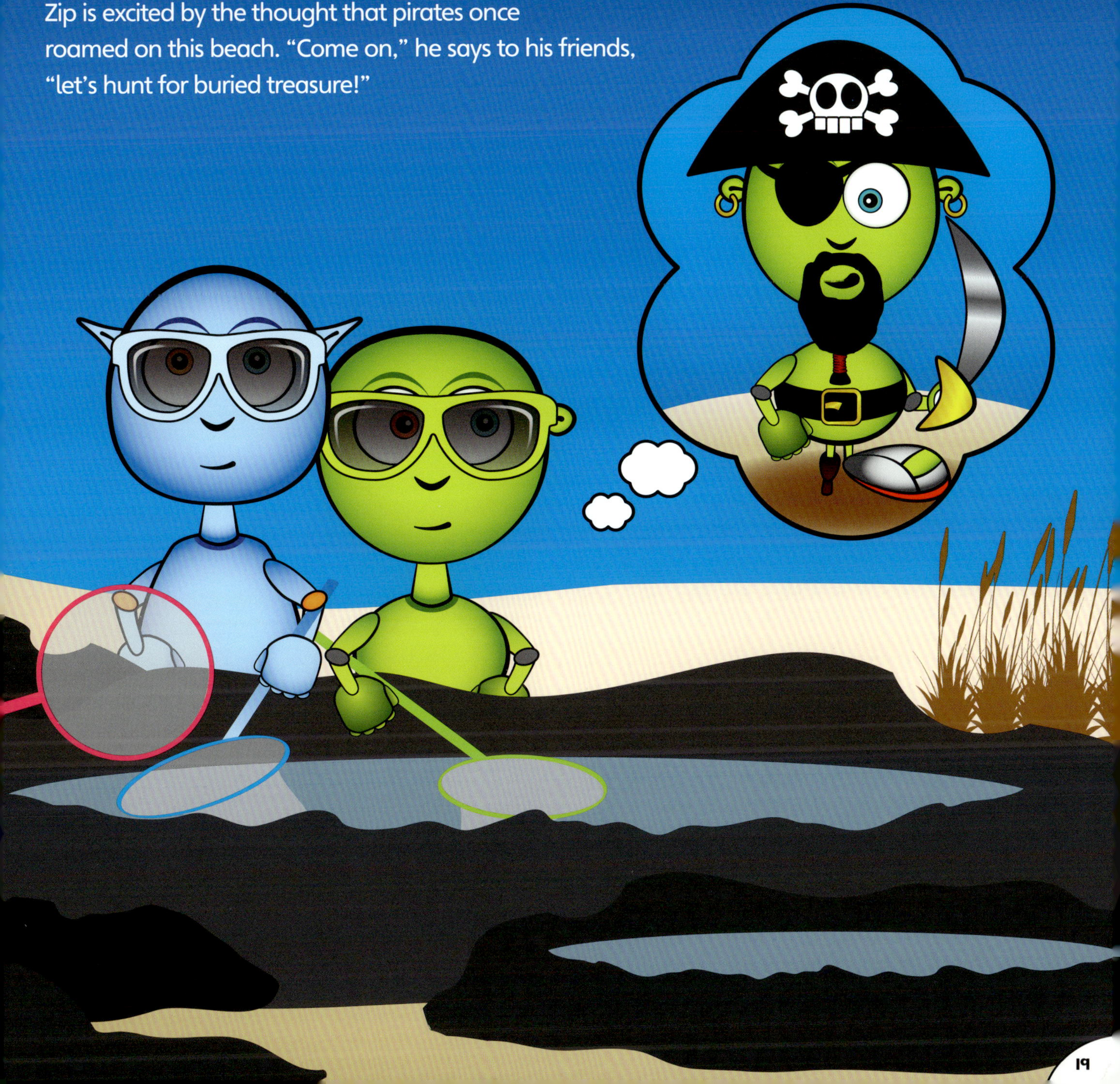

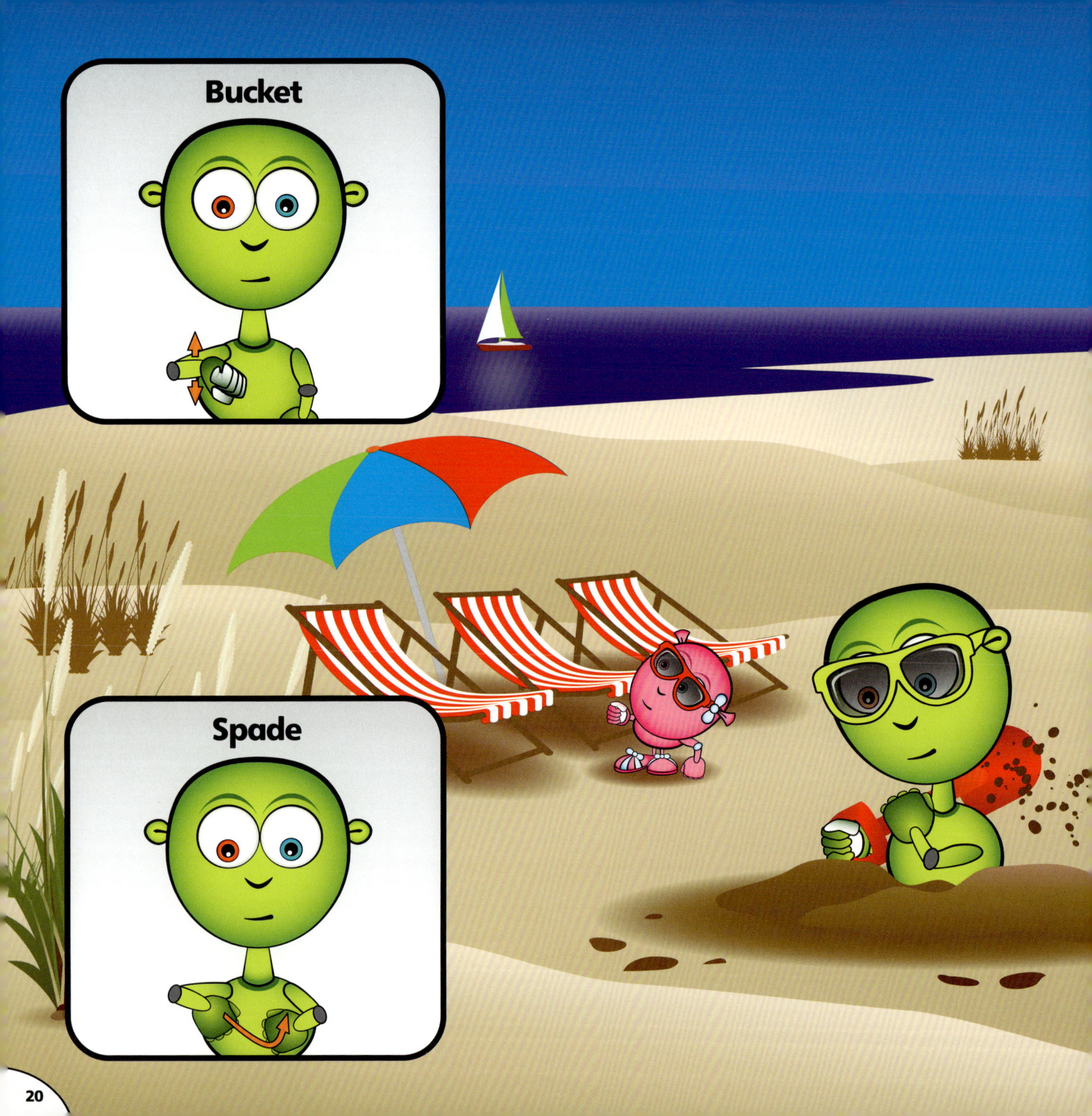
Bucket
Spade

The three friends start their treasure hunt. Zip gets out his bucket and spade and starts to dig in the sand.

"I'm going to look under deckchairs and umbrellas," says Pella.

"I'm going to download a pirate treasure map on my Zablet," says Statz.

Zip digs big holes all over the beach. “It says on my Zablet, that X always marks the spot where treasure has been buried,” says Statz. “Can either of you see an X anywhere?”

“Look,” shouts Pella, “there’s something sparkling in the sand over there.”

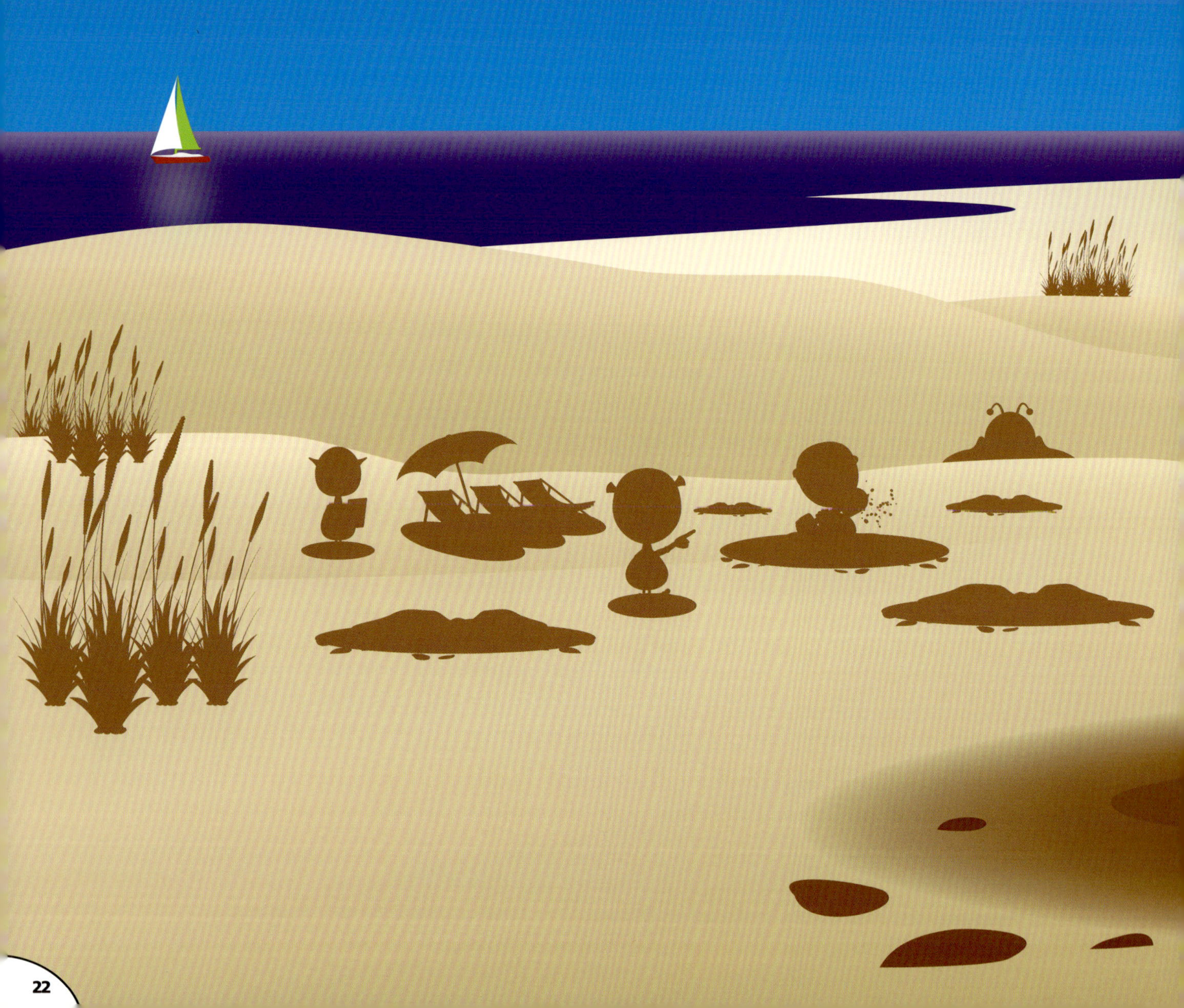

The friends run over to investigate and find three gold coins in the sand.

"Hooray!" shouts Statz, "we've found some treasure."

The friends are hungry after their day on the beach so they use their coins to buy some chips at a seafront café. They eat their food watching humans build sandcastles on the beach.

"It's a competition," says Zip. "The best sandcastle wins a prize."

"If we work together, we can build the biggest sandcastle," Statz tells his friends.

Zip, Statz and Pella have some time before they have to get back to the spaceship, so they decide to enter the competition.

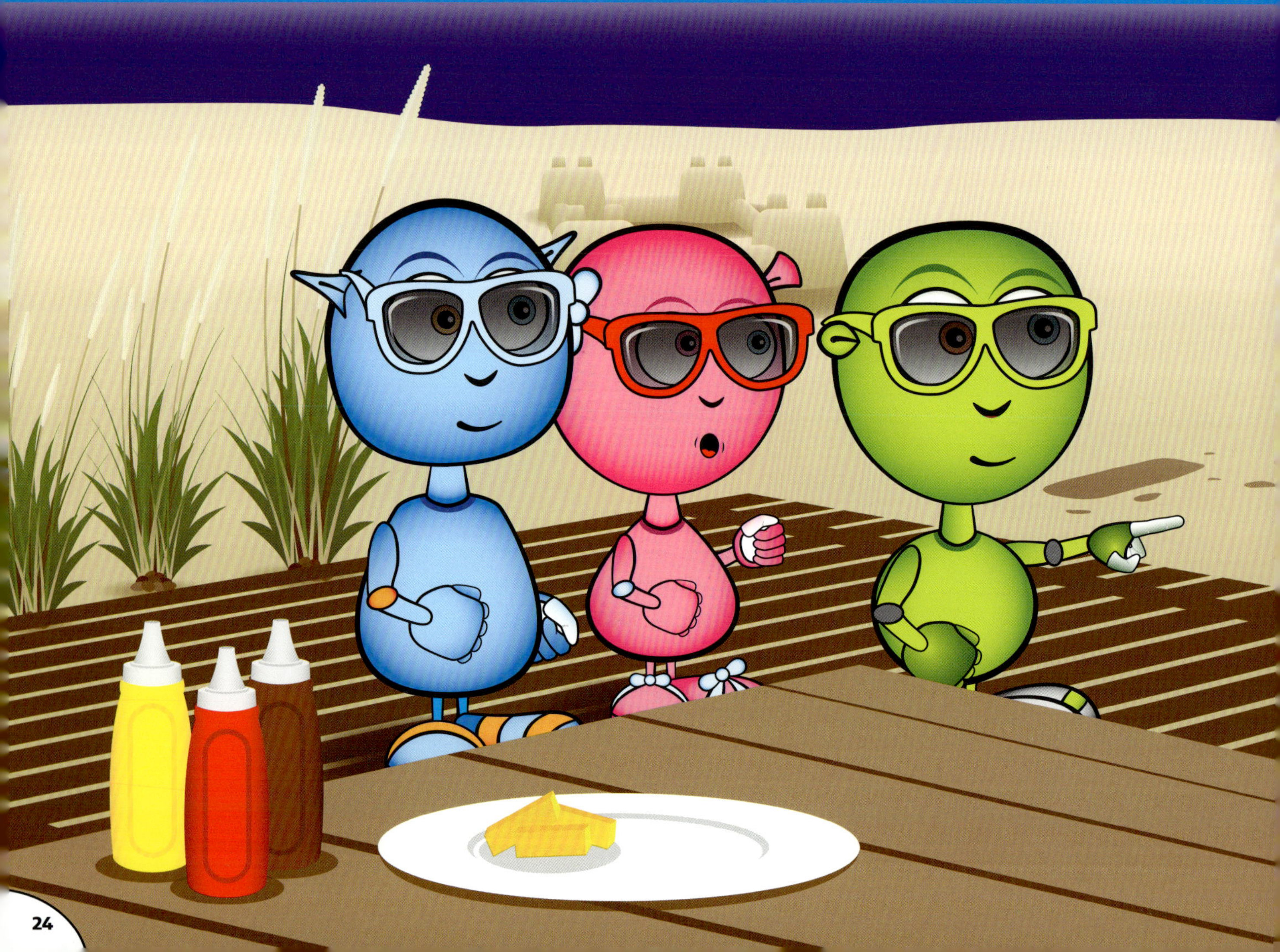

"This will be fun," says Zip.

"Come on Zip, bring your bucket and spade," says Pella.

They find a clear patch of sand and get to work.

Space School

Zip is having a great day at the seaside.
Take a look at Zip on the beach and see if you can remember the signs.

The friends use Zip's bucket and spade to build the biggest and best sandcastle ever. They are all very proud of their work.

"Stand there," says Statz. "I want to remember this." He takes out his Zablet and takes a photograph.

Suddenly the giant sandcastle starts to shake and crumble.

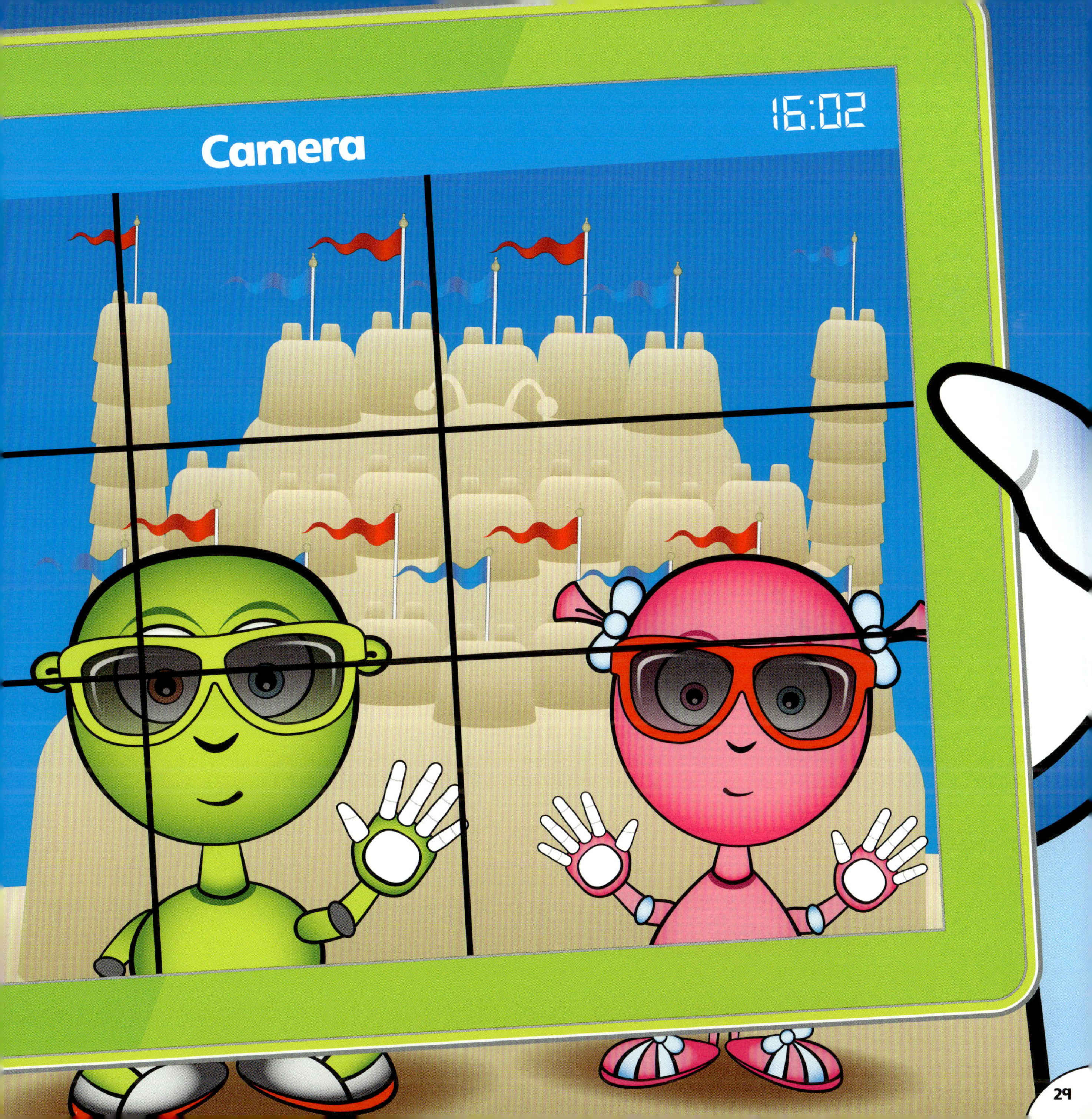
Camera
16:02

GOOBER!

Zip's Signs

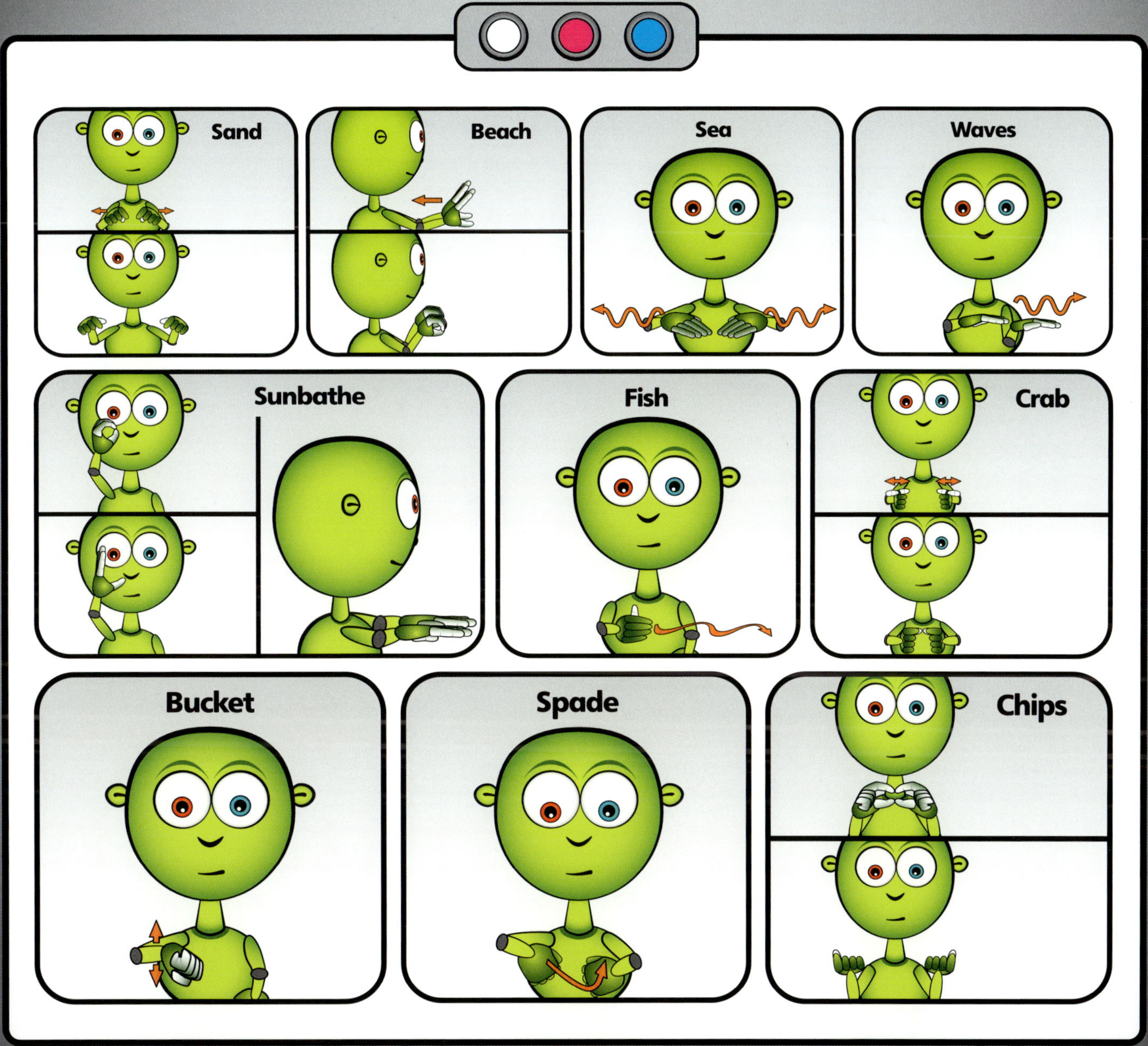

Fun things to do

Now that you have read all about Zip at the Seaside,
here are some fun things for you to do:

- **What would the seaside look like on planet Zee - draw, describe or write**
- **Create your own treasure hunt. What treasure will you bury?**
- **What would you pack for a day at the seaside?**
- **How would you feel if you went fishing and only caught an old brown boot?**
- **What would you do if you found some treasure?**
- **Teach a friend the signs for sand and sea**

First published 2013 by Signature

SignSpell® stories created by Signature
Designed and illustrated by Igloo Imaging Ltd.